AF322665

THIS SOLVES NOTHING

Official Edition
This Solves Nothing: You must learn from you
Published through IngramSpark
Copyright © 2024 by Radoslav Elijah Mladineo
All rights reserved.

ISBN: 979-8-8691-2891-1

THIS SOLVES NOTHING

You must learn from you

RADOSLAV ELIJAH
MLADINEO

PREFACE

"The art of writing is the art of discovering what you believe."

Gustave Flaubert

Dear reader,

Gaze upon this sizable wet rock in the endless space-time continuum, this statistical anomaly we call home with no definite purpose or meaning. Trapped within the intricate forest of life, as our forefathers and their forefathers before them, we live without an innate guidebook. So why aren't we all running around like headless Sartrean chickens?

An existentialist crisis certainly has merit, and yet we bother with trivial manners seemingly ignorant of reality when nothing matters! We work. We sleep. We repeat. At birth, a map is not handed to us, and yet one still exists?

Again, I ask you to gaze. Answers are only found through consideration. We make sense of reality through our own perceptions, governed by our experiences and observations. Philosophy reflects such the nature of our mortality.

Try then, in what I hope is genuine contemplation, to put pen to paper. Physically create your thought processes, life will unravel itself with time and dedication; this wildering jungle around us can feel a little more like home.

For most this process engages us in a very unique sense of introspection and self-expression. Writing forces us to stop wandering about, lost within the vibrant shrubbery, and think. The constantly moving train we get off and on everyday, combined with the relentless amount of stimuli we receive overwhelms our already hectic lives. As we age we find less and less time for a break in this frantic monotony, and even less time to give any thought on limited existence. But by walking the bridge between our chaotic life and the order we seek through writing, we gain clarity; not just about ourselves, but about the puzzling world around us. Both you and I can recognize the mystical aura associated with writing. It calms storms. Any intellect knows this. We may love living in denial, but as we write, truth stands in front of us. Eye to eye, its frigid breath caresses our skin, giving us a rare chance to reflect.

Through all my writing I have become no stranger to this phenomenon of forced reflection. Nothing has allowed me to ignore reality; in fact reality feels closer. Maybe I'm plain crazy, but writing took my hand and guided me through a place I had found myself lost in my entire life. Somehow it knew where to go, and I trusted it.

Though I must admit, for a while I had no idea where it was taking me. Told to "just trust the process," I kept writing and yet the world kept spinning. Expecting something, I got nothing. No veil lifted. No fog cleared. Every extra layer I added felt like I had accidentally spilled a mahogany paint bucket on a blank canvas. I didn't feel any deeper meaning in my work. While I did try my best, I didn't truly believe in the credibility of my own creation. A stranger to my work, I scoffed at its legitimacy. I'm no philosopher. I'm no Sartre or Freud.

This fallacy, this misconception holds our entire society back. Writing by any has merit because we write for ourselves! And yet we praise a small few; duped by their fancy words, and "deep" works of art, degrading our own tapestries of beauty. We cannot properly reflect on something we view as soiled or unqualified. Only by understanding our capability to create any reflective material for ourselves can we begin forming our own guidebook. Of course others can lean in and take inspiration, but only the author gains true revelation, their own personal philosophy of life. If we accept our own work we start to know where the hand may take us.

I don't blame anyone for feeling lost. In fact, I don't believe anyone truly knows every corner of the jungle at all. But we can make our own paths through it. We can find our way through the forest.

Writing plays a crucial role in the creation of each one of our personal guidebooks. A still moment for us to name our home.

-R. Elijah Mladineo

TSN I

If it's a theme you're looking for,
Look elsewhere.
If it's a message, sorry I'm unqualified.

I am no poet.
I am no author.
I am no stranger to,
Mediocrity.

This solves nothing
Nor answers any queries.
This quels no beasts
Of unkempt philosophy.

I am you,
You are me.
Both humans living in our,
Mediocrity.

Read and rest well
Over those who overthink.
Take heed of this obvious truth,
That this of all things
Solves nothing.

TSN II

Treachery.
Are any condonable?
To dine with the adversary
At the table with an ally
Who walks the path of
Judas before him,
With confident knowledge
Of his own adornment.

Why betray your master?
Why betray your friend?
Was it his temptation?
Was it easy?

Yet you ask for forgiveness;
A hand to save you.
But how can I whose hands
Held you for so very long?

TSN III

When that he does of which he speaks for him,
Is he at fault?
When that she does of which she speaks for her,
Is she to blame?
When countless morrows build the endless tomb,
That reach for stars of hopeless gleaming doom,
Who counts?
Who tries?
Who cares?

TSN IV

A glimpse was caught
Of the jewel that shown
A path to righteousness
Of heaven's own.

A man foretold
Of our perfection
A glimmering hope
Of redirection.

But to this man who once told me
That truth be found in reason,
I say begone, and frown upon
His earthly misconception.

TSN V

Demonic evil.
Divine innocence.
One of many dualities of mankind,
Of existence.
Seemingly everlasting is the conflict
Between two bitter opposites,
But truly of our own fabrication
For the sake of clarity.
We try to understand the incomprehensible.
We create something out of nothing.
Paradoxical reality shouldn't make any sense,
And yet it does.

Our own creation.
Our definitions.
Our dualities.

Death of a loved one
Brings about feelings
Impalpable to the inexperienced man.
Pure agony.
Despair.
Mankind's unmerciful fate pokes fun at our existence.
Finite mortality.
Innocence, contrary to this knowledge,
Means not yet knowing this hard-truth,
Blind to the limelight of fate.
Freedom from the heartache of life,

Death incarnate has yet to visit.

Yet inevitably
Innocence shatters,
Most fragile things do.

Each and every individual lens
Unravels the film of convoluted reality and defines it,
Not by what it is, but by what it is not.

Comprehension relies on definitions,
Definitions function on antipodes.
Ugliness lacks beauty. Peace waits for war.
These dualities provide us our
Sensible interpretation of life.
Yet, interpretations are subjective,
We base them on perspective.
No fact lay beneath the dark mist of evil.
Any man can see any deed as vile.
Evil only exists for the sake of goods creation.

This creation.
These definitions.
Such dualities.

When our own chalice of tranquility shatters
We are understandably overcome with unexplainable grief.
These thousands of little pieces,
Our fanatical desire to put the cup back together again.
As then,

To lament death. To fear death.
Oh! Our human emotions.
Don't we crave the simplicity of innocence?

Yet inevitably
Innocence will shatter,
All fragile things do.

But with this knowledge
Can I really expect
Correction in our acceptance?
Happiness requires hardship.
Strength requires weakness.
Grief requires first hand experience.
Such is unequivocally natural!

Still,

Refusal drives your creation.
Refusal drives our creation.
Refusal drives my creation.

TSN VI

If only I knew,
No.
If only I tried,
No.
If only I cared,
No.
If only you helped,
I'm still here.

TSN VII

This blanket sure is warm
And yet I prefer the cold.
I've thrown it off for no other reason
Then what seems to be my own self pursued
Temporary suffering.
I like the way goosebumps feel.

Is such vulnerability so unprecedented?

TSN VIII

A happy man sails off
Unchained by responsibilities.

A foolish man joins him.
A sad man watches them depart.
A young man aspires to one day be the happy man.
A dead man, well, is a dead man.

An old man scowls
At the unorthodox approach.
A funny man laughs
At what seems to be a joke.

An intellectual hypothesizes.
A genius theorizes.
A politician criticizes.

To what end can the conversation be
about a happy man and his quest
for a certain sense of agency?

And yet as we bicker
A wise man chuckles,
Knowing all too well
How round the world really is.

TSN IX

Almost as the endless sunshine rose above my head
Did night befall and rip to shred
The hope that I could have
A future among the clouds.

Though stars did delight me
It was daylight that did not fright me
Unmatched and untold beauty
That tortured me everyday.

I didn't know what to do
Laugh, cry or point at you
Who started this whole endeavor
Through means I can't explain.

And yet the sun rises again
As it always has
Upon this land.
So what has caused this perplexion?

I guess there's no one else to blame
For my hopeless self-inflicted
Mental pain,
But who's to say I'll ever change.

TSN X

This pattern never ends.
Infinitely stretching across:

My time
Your time
Our time

Yet we believe the present to be
So different and new
Why can't we sit down and reflect?

You must learn from you.

TSN XI

As a man of principle and order,
I appreciate a system.

Though even a perfect child you raise up
May lose your bet in this game,
A system provides the backbone we all need.

Our constitution
Our common laws
Such a magnificent foundation for success.

In this unpredictable world,
Appreciate a system.

TSN XII

Ha!
Try again.

The foe before me speaks
A peculiar tongue of shadows.
And yet we battle in a harmonious beauty!

As I attack, it defends.

As I injure, it heals.

But sure of my upper hand over a beast
That curses my kind, hunting opportunities,
I persist.
I am superior.

Ha!
I've played this game before.

This familiar twisted
Way to prove a point.
Can't you see my upper hand?

As I fail, you fail.

As I cower, you cower.

You've already lost this pointless battle

That I was made for, given the opportunity,
I win.
I control.

Ha!
Ignorant to my intelligence.

This foe can be quelled
Through human means.
But how can it still stand at my weakest!

As I quit, it succeeds.

As I suffer, it thrives.

This unexplainable drive it has over me,
Prevailing as I slumber, unresting,
It persists.
It proves me otherwise.

Ha!
What a fool.

The friend before me speaks
A tongue never meant for me.
And yet we exist in a harmonious beauty.

As I attack, it defends.

As I injure, it heals.

But sure of my upper hand with a beast
Completing my life, providing opportunities,
I persist.
We are superior.

TSN XIII

Just a compilation of lessons,
That's all life is.

They aren't hidden.
They aren't a mystery to solve.
You can touch them.

Laugh at the absurdity!
All for the sake of a lesson.

TSN XIV

Well isn't that ironic
I know you hate to say
Of our similar nature
Which you see here today

Consider this my friend,
Oh these joyful,
Our dissent wisely follows
The trends of content consideration.

It takes belittling,
Why should it happen again?

TSN XV

Stand all amazed
He speaks before you.

All can hear
Yet few do listen.

A tongue
Meant for us.
A gift
For us all.

Be not afraid.
You will not fall.

TSN XVI

It's a bold assumption to assume
Everything just works out.
Yet with all the trials and tribulations of life,
Don't we all have a story to tell?

It isn't a matter of good from bad,
Failure and success,
But an ability to tell
Your story.

Is there really anything more
Wonderful or beautiful than that?

You cannot go through life expecting
Anything other than what happens.
Fate defines us, right?

TSN XVII

Four yellow roses.
How, cliche.

It was so wondrous,
For a while at least.

Overgrown with weeds,
Torment and misery.

For a while at least.

Regrown for what?
More beauty?
That beauty died.

For a while at least.

Let us rewater the seeds,
Triumph and love.

For a while at least.

TSN XVIII

Another pattern for the sake of my own,
Boredom.
It's not complicated,
Focus elsewhere,

Is something I could say,
But you'd see through that, wouldn't you?

I can throw in some symbols,
I could add a message,
I easily write nonsense,

Is something I did say,
But I don't take that back, should I?

I'm not a liar,
I'm not a wiseman,
I'm easily humbled.

I like to bamboozle,
But I'm not an expert, is anyone?

I write to write.
You read to read.
They lie to lie.
We try to try.
So I may be not qualified,
But quite often I'm satisfied.

TSN XIX

Regret guides the imaginable,
Intangible and gray,
Overshadowing our every step
Until the end of day.

I have regrets, don't we all?
To fall and wreck it all.
But yet I'm driven to repeat
Cast down at God's feet.

But the greatest sinners of all
Are the ones who deny any fall at all.
They who believe in perfection,
They who martyr one's redirection.

Cherish your mistakes
As a treasure true to you.
Repent, repeat, I don't care.
At the least of all, just be aware.

TSN XX

I've stretched myself too thin.
It's over,
I can't continue!

Ripped into strands of gray pain,
My overly monotone motivation.

If your real world is this pain
Which I am the witness of,
Accept and continue.

If you quit they'll call you out.

TSN XXI

Carnal devotion
That blinds mankind.
Human nature
Among our time.

Bloodshot eyes
Of devilish substance.
Drunken man
Who mishaps judgements.

Fornication, lust and greed
Plant the seed of humanity.
Of which destroys us
Of which we utilize
Of which we all should heed.

Notes that tremble within my skin.
Of soul and beauty spread to kin.
That cures what we've always feared.
Among the living who suffer here.

Strokes that cure my own belief.
Of paint that stencils in our grief.
That many of us gather round.
To ponder what we have just found.

Music, art and creativity
Plant the seed of humanity.

Of which defines us
Of which we utilize
Of which we all should need.

Pointless violence
Dyes my hands.
Death incarnate
Across the land.

Unguided purpose
We all suffer.
Weeping heard
Inside oneself.

Pain, regret and purpose.
Plant the seed of humanity
Of which we fail
Of which we utilize
Of which join this stampede.

TSN XXII

When a man is happy with himself
Then all else falls into place.
A complete soul, unwarranted hardship
Turned away at his front door.

For his purpose he can ignore,
For his problems haunt no more.
A happy man in a happy state,
Reality, you can wait.

TSN XXIII

It is impossible for me to, in anyway express
Some of the most magnificent states of the human mind.
From which brings us closer to a temporal paradise
That cures our uncertainties.
Yet, while my hand can only be the messenger
Let this be clear:
It exists only because we who create it persevere
Through failure, exhaustion and desecration,
From the fires that ravage our forests,
Born be these wonders of the world.

TSN XXIV

If now we seek
What cures our mind,
Then maybe all will be well.

For when we rest
Our mind at ease,
We slumber erroneously.

You may assume
Correct or not
That I am now a critic.

But if I was
Then you would see
My hope well lost at sea.

VOLUME TWO

"Man is condemned to be free, nothing can save him from himself."

Jean-Paul Sartre

Are such opportunities for consideration not stifled by our own moral compass of biased legitimacy? Certainly the Cains and Grendels of the world, our monsters, feel inadequate; as the scapegoats of society their work is actively attacked, whether it be in the literary sense or the physical.

Is it only fair,
Must I allow,
Those others
Who we
Scapegoat?
The chosen few
Who lack any
New sense of
Proper identity.

In the untouchable heavens of human perfection above us lies a utopian world rid of mortal sin and self destruction; a striven for, everlasting paradise that society relentlessly pursues like a wolf on the hunt. Don't we all love to imagine this pure world of innocence? The elimination of mistakes and problems sparks the most profound, absolute joy inside of us. Who wouldn't want a warm, cozy, everyday vacation for all mankind?

Well, I'd argue our human nature seems to prove we don't want it. Can't we admit this reality seems a bit boring?

Perfection isn't very interesting.

Unconsciously or not, we have a desire for some chaos in

life, and monsters exist to fulfill that role. They ravage our order, they break our rules, and however illogical their existence, we create them, because they make life more interesting.

This fascination with mayhem stems from our innate nature to solve problems. Physically, as the underdogs of evolution, it doesn't take much to snap, break, and crush our frail little bodies. For this reason naturally we have had to rely on our keen intellect which perseveres through every challenge, and eventually finds its own way to win, even if not align with original expectation. It has kept us around today, and all of nature certainly feels our presence even with our physical disadvantages. Now, as an unstoppable force fueled by overcoming obstacles, we need our prey, a challenge to surpass. The wiring within us to look for or create a chase prevents a pointless, stagnant life; the pursuit stimulates us.

In Beowulf, an old English epic, the hero of the story found and quelled a murderous beast, Grendel, in an attempt to achieve said chase. He actively looked for a worthy foe, an opponent whose defeat would grant him fame and glory, and attained what seemed unattainable, besting the worst beast evil could throw at him. Though, the "beast" he destroyed simply demonstrated the natural desires of any wild animal, and if left undisturbed may have minded its own business. This monster didn't have to be a monster, but the hero of this story made it so. Beowulf desired to conquer an adversary, disregarding a reality where there wasn't one to begin with. And you must admit, the monster's existence made the plot a whole lot more interesting. No one wants a story without a Grendel.

My Monster, you and I
Solve my problems, then you'll fly.

His Monster, you shall be
Erroneously dying endlessly.

Their Monster, them and you
Solve my society, though it's not for two.

Now the existence of monsters, like Grendel, demonstrates an embarrassing absurdity of our hunts. We play a never ending game with ourselves to defeat life's inherent boredom, our one true adversary. We continue the game by creating finite order with rules made to be broken.

To not follow society is wrong, and to be oneself is unacceptable, right? Monsters are an example to those just joining this oppressive world of what happens when someone disobeys the master. They reveal our true situation in the world, and that uniqueness truly is a burden.

It is a fact that society punishes those different to normal ideals. Humanity looks down upon all minorities, only associating with those most similar to it. Facts, often using science and other kinds of evidence, defend our ideals. Facts define what it means to be normal, a loyal servant to the ungrateful masses, and what it means to be different. Facts are so heavily enforced that even the people it unjustly labels as monsters start to believe they are what society says they are. Society wants all to follow one certain set of rules and boundaries. It uses self-created truth to separate the unwanted from the wanted. They serve as a way to scare the masses into following so called truths, and prevent most from straying away from the norm.

Monsters are evil.
Monsters are strange.
You don't want to be a monster.

Yet a trap rigged for everyone lies beneath the false shrubbery of a fair system, and triggers with any possible excuse for a scapegoat. We like to believe in a just world, but would a just world set us up for failure? In Genesis 4 two brothers born of Adam and Eve, Cain and Abel, offered sacrifices to God and after Abel's was favored Cain slew his brother in jealousy.

Isn't God an all-knowing omnipotent being? Wouldn't he know full well that favoring one brother over another would end in this result? Certainly Cain tripped someone's wire, whether it be set by God, the devil or nature.

Monsters don't have to exist, but our ludicrous system defines them as such. Monsters simply break our duplicitous rules. Forget, rationalizing their creation or our system! The fine line between a hunter and the hunted only depends on who unluckily triggered a trap first. But it doesn't seem that we want to save our monsters. We don't care about the Cains and Grendals of the world because their tortuous existence paves way to the one true desire of mankind:

Not peace,
Not paradise,
Endless adventure.

TSN XXV

Eternal,
Among the many moons
Throughout this suffering
That doth consume.

If when I'm left at ease,
No grief,
I'll surely be appeased
At least.

TSN XXVI

Purple, brown, blue and gold,
Amenities of that royalty.
They sing the song
They dance along
The road of ignorant
Fantasy.

Oh look,
They enter here again!
Who welcomes them?
I wonder.

Do you?
Do I?
Go and say goodbye!
Back on that path of
Phantasy

TSN XXVII

For those who walk
Among those creatures,
Endless
Despicable
Evil features.
They are what we have always feared,
A mirror of us,
No longer here.

They may now look
A bit disfigured.
Hindered by a past of sin
And though their kin
Are same within
I promise you,
We'll give in.

TSN XXIII

Do not count the years going by,
Count the memories that have flown high.
For this you'll say in your older years,
"I have not one, but many tears."

And though you'll state
You wish not to wake,
I promise you, those pearly gates,
Are a promise in your fate.

But hold your head up high!
Wait a few years, then you'll die.
For now accomplish what you can,
Spread your anarchy across the land.

TSN XXIX

You've given me plenty of time
To contemplate, you are not wrong.
This journey I've pursued
Has left me soulless,
Yet he still walks past my door.
The effort in your godly name
Was it really all in vain?
This pain upon a man bears his weight
Upon a cane.
Unfulfilled deadly promises
Never-ending harnesses
Brought me nothing more
Then the skill of looking out my door.
So yes you may be right,
This procrastination hurts me.
What now I ask,
Aren't I out of time?

TSN XXX

I have yet to ask a question I have not the answer to.
And though some may call me a fool, I'll tell you of
its merit.
To be prepared, that is my song, but do I often wonder:
The glory in such purposeful thought, questions and ideas.

They who expect to be wrong are right, prepared in a
journey
Where the seas are calm. Yet among the many stars in
the sky
That shine, lost is any purpose that may
guide us towards success.

So while my answers may be wrong, stupid or lacking
meaning,
I truly am the winner of a life filled with some dreaming.

I must attest that my own ploy is nothing more than
hopeful.
But to that which I witness of,
Alas!
Some are lost.

TSN XXXI

Am I dreaming?
You surely ought to tell me
What's real and isn't.
For though I can count my fingers
My feet are many;
Too many footprints with too few steps.

It couldn't have been you,
I've watched your every move,
Your sprints across the sand
And tumble towards the water.
Though, as I closed my eyes you approached.
So maybe?

Defend yourself at least,
Put up a little fight!
You make this game so boring,

I ask again,
How then?
If it wasn't you or me
Surely there'd be less than three
Patterns among the earth.

TSN XXXII

You know what I know,
It's a lesson I should've learned.
That sheep ran off again,
Why don't I let it go?
It's not like this was unexpected,
Oh that sheep ran off again!
It's one of many,
And I've got plenty,
Sheep that stay and graze.

TSN XXXIII

Though I often wonder how to break the chains of solace,
I never have to wonder when the last day will befall us.
We live a life so few of us have reached the tallest
Mounds, and tumbled down
Right down mounds, into the hands of hounds.
Hounds of Hades right from his door
Eat our flesh right on the floor.
A pattern that I don't adore
Builds the chains nailed to the floor.
I wonder when
This home again
Will have these chains no more.

TSN XXXIV

I guess I do believe in fate
But not that wise man's silly fate
But fate sketched in the gate
Above the clouds which do I wait.
For who knows when I will ever wake
Will I ever see that gate
If fate guided me to such a state
Trembling, I shake.
I've made mistakes
Can I blame fate
For being late
I ain't walked straight
That's no debate
Don't hesitate
Go ahead, believe in fate.

TSN XXXV

Guide me towards an explicit nature
Where I can speak the words of birds
Who sing their mind,
Everytime.

I am flightless
I've dropped dead
Right out the sky
Right on my head.
I wander now and the sun does shine,
I am now prey to those divine.

They do circle round my path
A threat?
A savior?
I'll never ask.

I'm not up there, perched with the choir.
I'm right down here, close to the fire.
It burns yet I hold my in scream.
I cannot express my savior's game.

TSN XXXVI

Two men on a bench
Two feet apart,
The sun no longer rising.
One gets up and looks around,
The other sits in silence.
Both eyes speak words,
Your eyes speak none.
This reader gazes aimlessly.
Can you not be as these two men see?
Don't try to understand me.

TSN XXXVII

By another man
Who holds my hands,
My emotions are his sculpture.
The saddest man now the happiest,
Such joyful wonders that consume me.
You've placed them just as I
Right in the palms above the sky,
A mistake some call misplaced
But a choice I don't forsake.

TSN XXXVIII

Again I mention mediocrity,
To be a genius among the school
Yet drowning like a fool
Among actual geniuses.
A path so eviscerated,
It's bowels spread like carpet,
A higher goal stands over it,
Perfect as can be.
A simple quest
To be the best.
A timeless test
They do not rest.
They try their best
I can attest
They do invest
But are unknowing
Truly depressed.

Hearsay!
A jack of all trades and master of none
Has found what can fulfill a true man's fun.
Over a simple quest,
A pointless test,
A master just can't be won.

TSN XXXIX

Concisely put
I have been shook,
I am that raging monster.
That creature that I've always feared
Has seen itself in a dark old mirror
Uncovered by reflection.
No one else can label I
But myself and that child's cry of
Hypocrisy!

A shame I'll say, what has happened today?
Have I lost the right to proxy?

TSN XL

A morning dove
That once loved
Stands next to
A corpse.

A cry aloud
With gentle sound
Tears our hearts
In two.

For after all
This poor birds call
Is caused by
Our own hands.

And as it tries
To fly again
We take our
Aim and shoot.

TSN XLI

For the purpose of this debate
My faith shall be my philosophy.
As pointed out to me they might not quite align,
Which saddens me.
But I can only hope you'll allow it,
It's not as if you can respond.

I know that they aren't quite the same,
One builds the bridge
The other plays the game.
But I believe in the slight possibility
That they merge into a greater being of religious delicacy.

With careful thought I do proclaim
This selfish hypocrisy, not unique to me.
But it seems mortal man
Ignores my pleas for justice.
As if their word holds merit above yours!

Answer me then.

TSN XLII

If ignorance has bound you
Into one certain kind of individual,
Unwilling to take different paths in life.

If when you are approached
By that man in a rainbow sweater,
Who leans over and collapses.

If the cascade of unfortunate events
Has snowballed into personal chaos,
And your stiff moral bounds shatter.

If, and only if you accept
What you have become,
Can failure be yours.

TSN XLIII

I do believe these claims of mine
Are harmless pokes at literature.
Which we are taught to analyze
That ghostly sense of creed.

It may be true, I represent
A sinful man's great fallacy.

But I don't believe in any sense
That you know what I need.

I,
That man that has been told
The proper way to write.

I,
The man that has been sold
That proper way to read.

I,
A man who knows all men
Will fall with claims in hand,
Do believe these claims of ours
Are oughtly guaranteed.

TSN XLIV

A writing man
Is a fighting man,
Neither won nor lost
The test of time.

But once that writing man
Sits down to rest,
Overcome, not overwhelmed,
By pure happiness,
Then they who once
Fought and taught
Are caught, in a realization
That they have lost
Any desire
To continue fighting.

TSN XLV

Education by poetry requires educated poetry.
And though I do not claim
A level above any greats
For the sake of my own humility,
I do believe in such proper education.
But to those who seek what was
Never intended,
Look for that artist who reads
The strokes among a canvas
As accidental.

Purpose built on intent,
He who argues he is his own interpreter
Surely reads like a fool.

TSN XLVI

To harness what none can see,
Leads to all these pleasantries.
Emotions of the highest land,
Drawn on my palm
In a closed fist hand.

The balance that some may retain
Between total happiness
And pouring rain,
Seems to be apparent here
This genuine man
To all his peers.

He knew a sinner once
And his fist could not undo,
This emotional tear of pleasantries
That he shall always pursue.

TSN XLVII

Hope—
Fallen lies,
Stain our skies.

As have I?
My ignorance
Relies.

Bring about those
Chosen few,
Again I match your
Fearful news.

Bring about those
Chosen few,
Again I'll rally my
careful coup.

TSN XLVIII

How shall they be remembered?
Those known by many names,
Their diverse hands with bloody stains
Granting privilege in our name.

Praise or gratitude,
Let their be none in a world
Of ignorance and idiocy;
That praise will die.

But in a war-hungry world
Let the cost of man strike a bullet,
Lest their be any chance for
Gratitude in this hungry man's eyes.

Can we not remember and honor
While providing the needs that conjure
Our unity, or shall the pillaging continue?
This choice was born and lives in you.

TSN XLIX

This tranquil garden within an endless labyrinth,
The pinnacle of human ingenuity.
What do these gardeners do not allow?
Rapid overgrowth,
The weeds of unjust censorship.
If the blooming flowers suffocate
Opinions and conversation,
This balance becomes
A hellscape of chaos,
Not to be confused with evil.
Verbal communication plays
This crucial role,
Shaping our society by distinguishing
Between the wanted and unwanted.
It colors our perspective.
It realizes man's identity.
Its purpose serves to benefit man's knowledge,
Shall you then, tend to these crops?

You,
Gardener,
Nurture and keep this garden beautiful.

TSN L

We only have
So many years
To cherish,
And so it is
Pleasantly apparent,
To me at least,
These hundred years
Of hope and tears,
Must our grace
Be apparent here;
That when we
Wake in a state
Of hate, blatantly
Abhorrent to this
All so generous
Fate,
May we cherish
Our precursor
To those gates,
Awake and say
Your thanks.

TSN LI

Why do we often argue as a society
That one person is at fault for their own actions?
Is man not shaped by experience?
Is man not molded by his culture?

If we are born free of any
Innate nature,
Then to argue mankind created itself
By its own volition
Means to argue we are to
Blame for our own misdeeds,
Indeed?
Should we then,
Defend those who commit atrocities,
Not because they deserve it,
But because we have shaped them to do so?

Everyday is a repetition of our hopeless nature;
That we destroy because we have destroyed,
That we kill because we have killed.
I touch this pointlessness,
Gasping said uncertainty,
Aren't we all to blame?

Death surrounds us,
Yet we still point and punish.

Reflect.

Humanities acclaimed trend!

Is it,
Kill or be killed?
Will we live to see another day,
Crouched in corrupt fear,
Drowning in our disillusioned
Tears,

Those who fulfill the natural
Human desire are unnatural,
Yet a predator needs its prey,
Such a predator is natural.

TSN LII

I do hope that
We find some sense
Of urgency,
If do we ever
Lose our vibrant
Stature, the unlawful
Capture, this dull
And hopeless rapture.
Not all happiness can
Capture all joy,
It may be lost.

TSN LIII

Begone fair maiden
Dishevel all my years,

Begone brave warrior
Upheaving all my fears,

Begone wise elder
As I will adhere,

Begone these pillars,
Of which I hold so dear.

TSN LIII

Ship down the lane
On land but lost at sea
The captain yells and barks commands
Perhaps he's mocking me.

But will I ever truly know
How he stands to bold,
This child near to me
Falls and slips in snow.

TSN LIV

The ghastly sorrow
Released

Hanging there
Alone

The sad tree
bends

His only friend
Grown

Swings with the
Wind

The stench
Surrounds

Yet this lone
Girl

What has she
Found?

An opportunity.

TSN LV

This
Dream
Of mine,
Of another
Untouchable
Peace of Mind,
Ordered and set
Beyond perfect and yet,
Frustrating.

Please do
Manifest.

Though I attest,
I lack the proper rest
Be it may I'll fail that test
In this dream of mine,
Collapsing as I wake.

TSN LVI

What does he manifest?
A test.

Bound by the will,
Trapped and imprisoned
Resistance unattainable
Justice unimaginable
Lurking every hour
The harvester of nightmares,
My greatest fear:
The dominant discourse.

TSN LVII

Learn to struggle,
Learn to grow.
Accept your failure
Or you'll never know
That success is found
At the crossroads of
Application.

Play your hands
You have two,
Just one is stuck
Through and through
Repeating endless efforts.

TSN LVIII

The problem of the modern age
Is our inability to deal with opposition.
We are trying to wash away the dualities that define us.

It is those who disagree with us that we build off of.
When we build off of those who agree,
We lack our own opinion.

Of course dissent isn't always fun,
But there is a fine line.

People are going to disagree with you,
We cannot create a world where that wouldn't happen.

Of course my take on ridicule
May result in hardship,
But a mature setting helps us all grow.

TSN LIX

You tell me what I believe,
I tell you that you're naive.
Then I rest, proud and relieved,
Until you come and threaten me.

How can this be?

I tell you what you believe,
You just frown and throw a first at me.
It seems that I can just not perceive,
How we both were so deceived.

What do we really believe?

TSN LX

This author contradicts himself,
When winter comes he's ready.

Hold steady,
These contradictions tell more
Than meets the eye.

Gentle now,
That hermit may be wise.

TSN LXI

There he is,
Coward.
Make up your mind.

You really think
This limbo is subpar?

Curse this indecisiveness,
Shame to your uncertainty,

Curse my beating heart,
Eternal resting larceny.

TSN LXII

There he is,
Jester.
Your laughter makes me frown.

You really think
These jokes can cover pain?

Curse such lies,
Shame to your efforts,

Curse my joyful gaze,
Clapping hands and praise.

TSN LXIII

The honest folk have found
That those who share are never
Left with consideration.

Neighbors with these,
Monsters
Hounds
And bleeding gowns,
Friends with
Fiends and
Family among the
Ostracized.

Honestly are honest folk deserving?
Is what they share so unnerving?

TSN XLIV

He who perseveres has no fear of failure.
Look at his open arms,
The furrow of his generous gaze,
Does this figure inspire you?
He grabs both friends and foes
From a fall none deserve,
Comradery guided by principle.

The man who calls him the enemy
Is showered in his sleep
By flowers,
Not knifes.

Though those same hands which shower
Are scarred from the frightening
Teeth of every devouring soul,
He hauls up the mountain
With an equal and determined goal
Of granting one last surprised smile
To this apparent failure,
The failure he can only see through reflection.

TSN XLV

Thus ends my recollection
And tales of this empty city.

My works of all
In this chosen fall,
I ask for no certain pity.

But I do hope my hesitance
Hints at a sense
Of what I might have intended.

To those of all,
The gods and fallen,
Accept that this solves nothing.

Beware of another looming adversary:
Mediocrity.

Do you aspire for a life filled with mediocrities? Does that sound in any way fulfilling?

I believe it's fair to assume this word has fallen down the steps of respectability. Nobody wants to be called mediocre; that would be an insult. It's fascinating though, because mediocrity (the state of being mediocre) stems from *mediocris,* the classical Latin of middle, neutral. Why does it have such a negative connotation? Middle isn't bad, right?

When you take a step back past this negative connotation, it's clear that some modern dictionaries define the word true to its original meaning. The official *Oxford English Dictionary* states, "of middling quality, neither good nor bad, average." Yet, a quick Google search brings up a slightly different interpretation, "of only moderate quality; not very good," (*Oxford Languages). Merriam-Webster* takes this even further, "to a low quality, value, ability, or performance" It's interesting how this word develops over the spectrum of interpretation. *Oxford Languages* calls it "average work" and then calls such average "not very good." But the *O.E.D.* says that same average is, "neither good nor bad." It's quite the conundrum of definitions, and says a lot about our perceptions of averageness. It should be a very neutral term, but it is not at all and the consistency among dictionaries prove this.

It seems to me a tragically misunderstood development

of what success is found in the middle ground, a pinnacle achievement of your average accomplished man. Maybe it's not what everyone aspires for, but it's definitely not meant to intend failure. However it seems we frown upon averageness in this modern world as if it's nothing to be proud of. Such is our failure in understanding mediocrity.

Success is in the eye of the beholder; we cannot agree on what success means but we can agree it is broad and different for everyone. To me, success is not limited to being the best in one single field, but also in the pursuit of diverse skills and experiences. In some cases, success is found when somebody figureheads mediocrity, because by embracing mediocrity, we can enjoy a challenge while not being a limited person. Our definition of success may be different, but at the least of all our definitions of mediocrity should be the same.

This multifaceted word and concept (the two are tightly intertwined) prove the need for a clear reinstitution of what it means to be average, and why someone should be fine in being called mediocre. The word isn't necessarily an insult, it can have a positive connotation for some, but arguably it is at least neutral. We cannot allow further misconstructions that add to the biased opinions (which favor perfection) to exist within our definitions. At the bare minimum mediocrity shouldn't be failure.

But it can be very difficult to appreciate your own personal mediocrity. Not many can stand in the middle and say, "I am neither good nor bad, I am mediocre and I like that."

Do not misunderstand, I praise and encourage growth; there is always room to develop our skills and we should strive for it. But when you find yourself looking up at those chosen few, discouraged and beaten down, find your mediocrity commendable. After all, everyone is mediocre in something.

Naturally,
When you are pulled under the belly of Fate
Certain ignorance is inevitable,
But true recognition is found as you are torn
Limb from limb—agonizing in pain—
All the while gazing aimlessly
As your brethren partake more of the Fruit.

What is a trial without an obstacle?
There is constancy in this design.

So then how shall,
You live?
How shall,
We?

Live with joy.

Your substance, ambition
Shall be your flag.
Hold it high,
Accept the limitations of
Mediocrity, Failure and Success.

At the least of all just be aware,
This game was meant to be enjoyed.

We need to grow up if we ever want to save the victims of our literary mishaps! Believe in yourself even if it may solve nothing. For it is something, at least it is for you.

Though it's been said that
Man and men who
Spend such days at waste,
So shrewdly awake,

Can never find a place
Among the three strong
Figures at those pearly gates,

For the better I say
Then those at break.

From such
That state
Of hate
Near fate
This shrewdness takes
No breaks.

Farwell and thank you,

As for now,
This short lived life continues.

Why do I Write?

Within each of my hands I tightly hold two very different backgrounds. One side of my family are recent immigrants who came to this land of opportunity from Latin America and prospered through nothing else other than hard-work, persistence and tenacity. The other side of my family fought for this country's independence in the Revolutionary War; their sacrifices echo through the generations, instilling in me a profound sense of duty and patriotism.

The legacy bestowed by my diverse and resilient family history is one of struggle, triumph, and commitment. I see an opportunity to honor their sacrifices and carry forward not just as a writer, but as a thinker as well. The lack of supporting these innate foundations thereof makes us nothing short of boneless lard.

I hold a unique platform to champion the values of unity and understanding that are intrinsic to my heritage. In a time when political discourse and polarization are commonplace, I believe that my diverse background equips me with the natural ability to navigate differing perspectives with empathy and open-mindedness. I aim to be a bridge-builder who fosters communication and cooperation among this society of conviction. I hope I can be a leader putting a stop to, as John P. Shanley would say, "courtroom culture."

This amalgamation of backgrounds puts me at the crossroads of the complexities and beauty in the American mosaic. We are all different and when we appreciate it our goals reveal themselves. Writing is just one of the stepping stones in my path towards service to the country in the armed forces, much like my grandfather's before me. It never has, and never will be easy or handed to me, but I believe loyalty and trust will guide me. As I decorate a veteran's grave, or honor tradition through Scouts I always see countless examples of America providing for the diligent. I've got both ends, and when I pull them close I see an American possibility; appreciation guides my adventure.

Alpha and Omega
The Deus of the Machina
Present such terms
Of hoarded souls,
Boast these hands
Of Mortal Woes.

Glee and Bliss
Do hail the uncertainty
To which we find our
Purpose,

Let glory in your
fate arise,
As gentle sorrow
Fills our eyes.

NOTES

The poetry of *This Solves Nothing: You must learn from you* is untitled, and largely sorted chronologically by Roman numerals (TSN __)

TSN II, III and IV were first written as study session material for a poetry unit within a sophomore English class, and after encouragement to continue from peers the work continued until TSN XLVII for the original edition published on Feb 1st of 2024.

It is not intended that this text shall ever contain page numbers, a table of contents, or be reordered in any shape or form (excluding next editions by the author). *This Solves Nothing: You must learn from you* is a single text in of itself.

A special thanks must be made to New Trier Township High School for providing valuable opportunities for students alike.

AGAIN, FAREWELL

"The closeness everything depends on the closeness with which you come, and you ought to be marked for the closeness, for nothing else. And that will have to be estimated by chance remarks, not by question and answer. It is only by accident that you know some day how near a person has come.

The person who gets close enough to poetry, he is going to know more about the word belief than anybody else knows, even in religion nowadays. There are two or three places where we know belief outside of religion. One of them is at the age of fifteen to twenty, in our self-belief. A young man knows more about himself than he is able to prove to anyone. He has no knowledge that anybody else will accept as knowledge. In his foreknowledge he has something that is going to believe itself into fulfilment, into acceptance."

Education by Poetry
Robert Frost